The Water Cycle
Frost, Helen

Yellow Umbrella Books are published by Capstone Press
151 Good Counsel Drive, P.O. Box 669, Mankato, Minnesota 56002
http://www.capstone-press.com

Library of Congress Cataloging-in-Publication Data
Curry, Don L.
     The water cycle/by Don L. Curry.
     p. cm.
     Includes index.
     ISBN 0-7368-0727-6
     1. Hydrologic cycle—Juvenile literature. [1. Hydrologic cycle.] I. Title.
GB848.C87   2001
551.48—dc21   00-038157

     Summary: Describes the water cycle in simple text and photographs.

Editorial Credits:
Susan Evento, Managing Editor/Product Development; Elizabeth Jaffe, Senior Editor;
     Jessica Maldonado, Designer; Kimberly Danger and Heidi Schoof, Photo Researchers

Photo Credits:
Cover: Stephen Simpson/FPG International LLC; Title Page: Unicorn Stock Photos/Jim
Shippee (top left), International Stock/Hal Kern (top right), Index Stock Imagery
(bottom left), Unicorn Stock Photos/Ed Harp (bottom right); Page 2: International
Stock/Patrick Ramsey; Page 3: Unicorn Stock Photos/Gerald Lim; Page 4:
Chuck Mitchell; Page 5: Unicorn Stock Photos/Jim Shippee (left), International
Stock/Kadir Kir (right); Page 6: International Stock/Hal Kern; Page 7: International
Stock/Robert W. Slack; Page 8: Unicorn Stock Photos/Andre Jenny; Page 9:
Jim Cummins/FPG International LLC; Page 10: Index Stock Imagery; Page 11:
Richard Price/FPG International LLC; Page 12: International Stock/Dario Perla;
Page 13: Unicorn Stock Photos/Ed Harp (left), Unicorn Stock Photos/Jim Riddle (right);
Page 14: Visuals Unlimited/D. Cavagnaro (left), Visuals Unlimited/Joe McDonald (right);
Page 15: International Stock/Bob Firth

Art on page 16 by Shelley Dietrichs

1 2 3 4 5 6 06 05 04 03 02 01

THE WATER CYCLE

BY DON L. CURRY

Consulting Editor: Gail Saunders-Smith, Ph.D.
Consultants: Claudine Jellison
and Patricia Williams,
Reading Recovery Teachers
Content Consultant: Jody Byrum, Science Writer

Yellow Umbrella Books

an imprint of Capstone Press
Mankato, Minnesota

It is raining.
Rain is big water drops.
Don't get wet!

The rain has stopped now.
The sun begins to shine.
The heat of the sun
makes things warm.

Look! Do you see the steam
on the basketball court?
The sun is heating the rain water.
The sun's heat is turning some
of the rain water into steam.

4

Steam is made up of a lot
of tiny water drops.
When you boil liquid
or breathe out on a cold day,
you see steam.

Steam is very light.
Steam is so light that it moves
up high into the sky
and forms clouds.
Because the steam in the clouds
is so light, clouds float.

Clouds collect water drops
until they become dark
and very full.

When clouds get too full,
they drop some of the water.
When it is warm, clouds might
drop water as rain.

On a very cold day, clouds
might drop the water as snow.
Snow is frozen, or solid, water.
Snow can be a lot of fun!

Water drops from clouds fall
to different places on Earth.
Some of the water that drops
from clouds falls
onto sidewalks and streets.

Some of the water
that drops from clouds
soaks into the ground
to water plants and trees.

Some of the water that drops from clouds falls and flows into rivers, lakes, and oceans. Animals drink the water.

The sun once again warms
some of the water dropped
from the clouds. This water
changes into steam and rises
to become clouds again.

Water falls from the clouds down to the earth, turns to steam, rises to make clouds, and then falls again. This process is called the water cycle.

Words to Know/Index

boil—to heat a liquid until it bubbles and gives off steam; page 5

cloud—a white or gray group of tiny water drops and dust in the air; pages 6, 7, 8, 11, 12, 13, 14, 15, 16

cycle—a complete set of events that happens again and again in the same order; page 16

Earth—the planet on which we live; pages 12, 16

frozen—solid at a very low temperature; water freezes at 32 degrees Fahrenheit (0 degrees Celsius); page 11

liquid—something wet that flows freely; page 5

rain—water that falls to the earth as drops; pages 2, 3, 4, 8, 16

sidewalk—a path for people to walk on along the side of a street; page 12

solid—something that keeps its shape; page 11

steam—a vapor made up of water drops and water in the form of a gas; pages 4, 5, 6, 15, 16

Word Count: 281
Early-Intervention Levels: 13–16